THE COMPLETE NICARAGUA TRAVEL, RETIREMENT, FUGITIVE & BUSINESS GUIDE

The Tell-It-Like-It-Is Guide to Relocate, Escape & Start Over in Nicaragua 2018

Claude Acero

Copyright © 2018 Copyright - by Claude Acero All rights reserved.

License Notes

This book is licensed for your personal information and enjoyment only. This book or any portion thereof may not be reproduced or used in any manner whatsoever without the express written permission of the publisher except for the use of brief quotations in a book review. If you would like to share this book with another person, please purchase an additional copy for each recipient. If you're reading this book and did not purchase it, or it was not purchased for your enjoyment only, then please return to your favorite retailer and purchase your own copy. Thank you for respecting the hard work of this author.

Disclaimer: The author of this ebook is not liable for the actions of any reader of this book; all the information is of the author's personal opinion

Chapter Overview

Introduction & About Me

Nicaragua in a Nutshell

Personal Experiences

The Lay of the Land

Climate and Seasons

Religion in Nicaragua

Nicaraguan Food

Arriving in Nicaragua and Transportation

Immigration and Visas

Types of Residencies

The Application Process

A Word About the Economy

Buying Real Estate in Nicaragua

The Judicial System and Hiring a Lawyer

Business Ideas Suitable for Nicaragua

Trivial Information & Location

Fugitives Escapists Paradise Nicaragua?

International Healthcare

Conclusion and Afterword

Introduction & About Me

My name is Claude Acero and I would like to extend a warm greeting to you all. After spending over three years in Nicaragua, I am now sort of a modern drifter, peddling between Central America, Miami, and sometimes Spain.

This book is not written as a competition to all the travel and retirement books about Nicaragua that are currently on the market; rather, the content of this book is focused on relocation and key aspects of international living in Nicaragua. The idea of this information is to make a new "untraditional" lifestyle in one of the most diverse countries in Central America more self-supporting. I also hope that this guide will motivate readers to pursue their dreams and happiness abroad. I'd like to thank the readers for their time and interests, and wish future expatriates the best of luck in all their endeavors!

If you think this books sounds pretty "factual", I suggest you look at my new "lighthearted" book which covers most of Central America, but has a completely different approach to the material:

Available as an ebook on various book platforms:

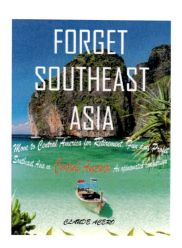

Nicaragua for Expats in a Nutshell

To most foreigners this country is still considered as a somewhat exotic place, and many things in this country may take a certain "learning curve". Fun can be had in Managua and Granada, they're a small city with many long-time expatriates. In Managua, it doesn't take much research to find all the fun and the goodies, all sorts of entertainment is available.

Nicaragua is a very cheap country for almost everything, food and housing prices are considerably lower than those in the United States and Europe. Even compared with Guatemala or Honduras, Nicaragua is still the most inexpensive country in the region.

Nicaragua can be a good choice for anyone interested in opening a business because you can have many businesses that in other countries would normally require a license.

Personal Experiences

Marcus' Experience

Marcus, a young guy from France, but already a seasoned expat, a travel guide writer and a friend of mine, is also not a stranger to relocating to exotic places, having lived in Spain, Argentine, Peru and Guatemala. He makes the most of any new home country. He started volunteering for a Madrid based NGO to have a free place to stay and he gains employment as a carpenter as his situation allows. He gets to know other foreigners and becomes good friends with a few. He gets involved in volunteering and religious groups. He got into something I have rarely seen, - he found a girlfriend and and probable future spouse from Spain! But Marco still wasn't happy enough, he tried living in various countries and places before he and his Spanish girlfriend ended up in *San Juan Del Sur*, Nicaragua where he's renting a large house nicely surrounded with some very influential neighbors. I am not completely aware how he is financing his lifestyle, but his latest idea is founding his own non-profit organization.

Diana - from Costa Rica to Nicaragua

Diana comes from a respectable family and her parents are friends of mine. Diana and Mat, both from L.A. have been actively traveling together to Europe and the Dominican Republic. I didn't know them socially until by chance I met these "kids" at the airport. We kept in touch and in 2009 the newlyweds moved to San José, Costa Rica where they tried to start a modern language school, but the truth is, their business had all kind of legal problems from the day they opened. A year later they had enough of Costa Rica's crime and insecurity, and decided to settle in neighboring Nicaragua. Mat, nevertheless, never felt quite at home in Central America, so they ended up estranged, each person going their own way.

Diana is a writer and artist living now in Granada with her new "novio" and two dogs who think they're people. She is successfully buying small artworks and ships them directly to the States making decent money on Etsy. Just recently she decided to change her location, she's thinking of moving north to the city of *Estelí* because of the unbearable climate and electricity cost in *Granada*; an understandable position since utility costs in this country an be a rude awakening. However, this country suits her well, - it looks like she found her little "privacy & freedom" there, and I must mention, I cannot bow low enough when I see a talented young person taking the plunge and then becoming successful in a relative short period of time.

The Lay of the Land (The Facts)

The Republic of Nicaragua is the largest country in the Central American isthmus. It has a total area of 130,370 square kilometers, comprising of 119,254 square kilometers of landmass and 10,380 square kilometers of water bodies. The coastline on both Atlantic and Pacific sides together is 910 kilometers. The country is bordered by Honduras in the North and Costa Rica in the south.

The landscape of Nicaragua may be divided into three distinct parts: The Pacific Lowlands, a flat region with a line of active volcanoes, extending 75 kilometers inland

The Central Highlands, a triangular area with rugged mountain ridges. The highest point is *Mogoton*, at 2438 meters.

The extensive Caribbean lowlands, covering about 50 percent of the country's landmass. Tropical rainforest covers about 20,000 square kilometers of this region.

The rift valley caused by the volcanoes in the Pacific lowlands host Lago de Managua and Lago de Nicaragua, the two largest freshwater lakes in South America. The *Río Tipitapa*, the major river of Nicaragua, flows through this region. The rugged mountain peaks of the Central Highlands abound in oak and pine forests.

The largest city and capital of Nicaragua is Managua, situated on the Pacific lowlands. The other major towns are *Esteli, Matagalpa* and Granada in the Pacific lowlands, and *Bluefields and Puetro Cabezas* in the Caribbean lowlands.

Ometepe Island

Climate and Seasons

Most of Nicaragua can be considered as hot and "muggy". However, the climate varies more from elevation than from the seasons. Rainfall fluctuates greatly in Nicaragua and is seasonal; the rainy period runs from May through October. The Caribbean lowlands are the wettest section of Central America, receiving between 98 and 256 inches (250 and 650 centimeters) of rain annually. The east receives heavy annual rainfall and can even see serious flooding during the rainy season, while the west is drier year-round.

December and January are the coolest and most refreshing month, with good clear weather, starry skies at night, and warm enticing days. Up in the mountains north of *Esteli* the temperature might drop to a brisk 16 C (60 F), but along Lake *Cocibolca*, int the capital, and on La Isla de *Ometepe,* nights during this period are still a balmy 22C (70F), and throughout the country, daytime temperatures are around 32C (88F). This Nicaragua is at its best: Summertime, or el *verano* (dry season), is mostly verdant, crisp and colorful.

But February-May, temperatures slowly climb until you are staying in you own sweat, and the damp heavy air begs for the release of a thundershower that never comes. By April, daytime temperatures are frequently 41 C (105F) with little relief at night as temperatures lingering around 25 C (75F). Your opinion of just how hot Nicaragua is might be radically readjusted during this period, especially when the sun-baked dust settles into every nook and cranny of your body and home. On or about May 15, the long-awaited first rain fall, and Nicaragua enters its wet season (*el invierno*), which lasts until November (in the more arid north and west) or December. The rains let up only once, for approximately two weeks in mid-August. This canicular signals the harvesting of the first crop and planting of the second, and it is typically a two-week period of bright sunny skies and no rain whatsoever.

Language

Spanish is now the official language of Nicaragua and is spoken by more than 70 percent of the population. Most Spanish speakers live in the Pacific lowlands and central highlands. Grammar and usage follow Central American forms, which has some distinct differences from formal Spanish in Spain. The British presence in Nicaragua introduced many English words to the Spanish speakers, particularly in western Nicaragua. Likewise, American slang from the periods in which U.S. Marines occupied Nicaragua, as well as hip-hop and rap music has made its way into the vernacular of Spanish speakers.

Religion in Nicaragua

Religion is a significant part of the culture of Nicaragua and forms part of the constitution. Religious freedom, which has been guaranteed since 1939, and religious tolerance is promoted by both the Nicaraguan government and the constitution. Religious leaders are expected to lend their authority to important state occasions, and their pronouncements on national issues are closely followed. They can also be called upon to mediate between contending parties at moments of political crisis. Although Nicaragua has no official religion it is nominally Roman Catholic.
Practicing Roman Catholics are no longer the majority and are

declining while Protestant groups and Mormons are growing rapidly have been growing since the 1990s. There are also strong Anglican and Moravian communities on the Caribbean coast. Roman Catholicism came to Nicaragua in the 16th century with the Spanish conquest and remained, until 1939, the established faith. Protestantism and various Christian sects came to Nicaragua during the 19th century, but only during the 20th century have Protestant denominations gained large followings in the Caribbean Coast of the country. Popular religion revolves around the saints, who are perceived as intermediaries between human beings and God.

Most localities, from the capital of Managua to small rural communities, honor patron saints, selected from the Roman Catholic calendar, with annual *fiestas*. In many communities, a rich lore has grown up around the celebrations of patron saints, honored in August with colorful, often day-long processions through the city. The high-point of Nicaragua's religious calendar for the masses is neither Christmas nor Easter, but "La Purísima", a week of festivities in early December dedicated to the Immaculate Conception, during which elaborate altars to the Virgin Mary are constructed in homes and workplaces.

Nicaraguan Culture

Like many Hispanic cultures, family relationships are highly valued and include relatives beyond the nuclear family unit. The word *compadrazago*, which literally means co-paternity, indicates the bond among children, parents, grandparents, and godparents.

With a high fertility rate, households are large—generally comprised of six to eight persons—and include grandparents and aunts and uncles. In rural areas, large families are regarded as a blessing: parents have help with chores and farm work. In urban settings, large families with extended kin allow for creative ways in which to house entire families, despite the space constraints of city living.

Religious Beliefs

Officially, Nicaragua is a secular state; Roman Catholicism arrived in Nicaragua with the Spanish conquest in the sixteenth century and remained the established faith until 1939. Most Nicaraguans are Roman Catholic, but many blacks along the coast, belong to Protestant denominations.

Nicaraguan Food

Typical Food: A traditional Nicaraguan meal consists of eggs or meat, beans and rice, salads of cabbage and tomatoes, tortillas and fruit. Also common is *gallo pinto*, a blend of rice and beans. Other typical dishes include *bajo*, a combination of beef, greens ripe plantains and yucca; also, *vigorón*, yucca served with fried pork skins and coleslaw. Nicaraguan food, like that of all "Mesoamerican" peoples, is based on corn and beans.

Music!

Nicaraguans love music everywhere! Restaurant staff, taxi drivers, hotel employees will "pump it up" as soon as a single guest arrives or a customer is approaching from across the street; it happens regardless, and if you ask to turn it down just a little you probably will be ignored or they will wait a few minutes and turn it up again. Young people are much into *reaggeton*, *latin pop* and hip-hop; traditional Nicaraguan music - *folclorico, chicheros, marimbar* guitar tones is often heard in better restaurants and family reunions.

Arriving in Nicaragua and Transportation

Unless you arrive via Pan-American Highway through Mexico, plan to land at Managua´s Augusto C. Sandino International Airport (MGA). At the airport you can rent a vehicle, meet your guide, or catch buses north or south. Managua´s fancier hotels offer bus service from the airport and in Granada they have a few private shuttle services for personal airport transfers.

Transportation

Traveling between cities by public bus is the best way to get a sense of what Nicaragua is like - and what being Nicaraguan is like – but if you are on a limited time frame, it is not the most efficient way to go. In that case, several companies rent vehicles at the Managua airport, where you can strike a deal for a short-term or several-week rental. You can also choose to hire a car and driver through your hotel or real estate agency to facilitate getting around.

City of Granada

Immigration and Visas

Short Term Visas

Every visitor to Nicaragua must possess a passport valid for six months beyond the date of entry. Upon entering the country most visitors will be granted a three-month tourist visa. But visitors from certain countries require a visa in advance of arrival. These include: Afghanistan, Albania, Bosnia, Colombia, Cuba, Haiti, India, Iran, Iraq, Lebanon, Libya, Nepal, Pakistan, the People´s Republic of China, the People´s Republic of Korea, Somalia, Sri Lanka and Vietnam. Longer Visas are also granted for special purposes like work, study and similar reasons, but their requirements are more stringent, and some – like a student visa – require a substantial deposit beforehand. For that reason most students usually just arrive on tourist visas and avoid the hassle and cost.

It´s improbable that any fact-finding trip would last longer than three months, but travelers who require an extension to their three-month tourist visa can do so during business hours at the Immigration "kiosk" in the *Metrocentro* Mall or by visiting the main office of immigration.

Immigration and Entrance

The easiest way to begin is to enter Nicaragua on a plain tourist visa (you get a 90 day tourist stamp upon arrival, unless you are from one of the restricted countries, it´s easy renewed) and deal with getting a longer-stay visa once you´re in the country. Make sure not to lose the immigration card they give you at the airport when you arrive, as you must present it again on departure.

While you could probably stick around on a tourist visa, not being official will eventually hinder your lifestyle in ways that matter, like being able to open a business or checking bank account, (a savings account is fairly easy with some banks on a tourist visa) , getting connected with a phone or cable TV company, and come and go as you please. So while it´s ok to start your investigation and exploration on a standard three-month tourist stamp, but it's probably not an acceptable solution for the long term.

At the immigration office (directions mentioned above) they will extend most types of visas. You pay less than a Dollar for the form, and you must present photocopies of your passport information page and the page with your visa. Many travelers in *San Juan del Sur* prefer just to take a bus over the Costa Rican border and return the same day on a fresh new tourist visa.

All requests for resident visas must also be made at the Office of Immigration in Managua (they are working on a promising website for e-applications)

Types of Residencies

There are two main types of residency visas and two types of retiree resident visas, when obtained, they grand your officialdom in the form of a so called *Cédula* (residency card).

Note, the permanent residence visa (*residente permanente*) and the investor's visa (*residente inversionista*) are nearly identical, with the exception of one additional requirement for investors, and both require a number of authorized and translated documents. In essence, to become a resident you have to prove that you do not pose any significant health risk, that you won't become an economic burden, and that you are not a criminal. Doing so will take proper documentation, and you will need to invest time and effort in obtaining, copying and notarizing the required documents. Having a reputable Nicaraguan business partner greatly streamlines your way through the system. As does having a bank account that makes it clear that your presence in Nicaragua will be an economic asset, not a liability. The government is trying to attract investors and is not overly inclined to facilitate the entry of those they call "hippies" (*mochileros*). Furthermore, two types of retirees are now recognized, - a governmental monthly pension of USD 900 (this may amount will fluctuate each year) or any proof of income which also can be generated abroad *(Residente Rentista* min. USD 900 a month) However, a company salary from abroad does not qualify, but private income from investments, stocks, bonds and other types of revenue is acceptable.

Temporary and Permanent Residence Visas

This is the first step for most expats interested in remaining in Nicaragua for more than three month at time, and is thus the most common *cédula* for which foreigners apply. Once you have renewed your temporary residence visa three times, you can apply to have it converted to a to a Permanent Residence Visa. Officially, once you have met all the administrative requirements listed below and your application has been successfully accepted, you can expect to receive the documents within two weeks, in practice it takes often longer than that. If you are already married to a Nicaraguan, it is worth asking if you can go straight to permanent status. Although officially this is prohibited, practice shows it is not. Your birth certificate, criminal record, marriage license, and health certificate must all be authenticated and translated.

There are two ways to do this and no clear consensus as to which is more straightforward. The government of Nicaragua specifically requests that you have your documents notarized and translated before moving to Nicaragua via the Nicaraguan consulate nearest you (as you'd have to appear in person at some point during the process). The second way is to have your paperwork notarized and translated at your nation´s embassy in Nicaragua. The U.S. embassy will notarize any document except a police report for American citizens.

Following is a complete list and description of all necessary documentation.

Request for Temporary Resident Form: You can purchase this at the Office of Immigration for under USD 5.

Passport Photos and Passport:
You must provide two passport photos facing forward and with a white background, available at any number of photo and office shops throughout the country. As a foreign resident, it´s a good idea to keep a stock of passport photos in your possession at all times, as much official business seems to require them. If you have a good-quality printer or scanner, it´s a good idea to scan one of them so you can print extras at will. You must also provide photocopies of every page of your passport with the exception of pages that have never been stamped at all. Photocopy the cover as well. Always carry your passport to any official meeting or inquiry.

Proof of Income / Funds:
The idea is to prove you are able to sustain yourself economically without becoming a burden on the government of Nicaragua. Officially you are required to provide a formal letter written on company letterhead of Nicaraguan company or corporation with whom you are employed, and that company must be registered in the Nicaraguan government´s *Registro Mercantil* (business registry). In practice, would-be foreign residents wind up proving they can sustain themselves in Nicaragua by revealing information about their checking and savings accounts as well as sources of income from retirement pension plans or IRA´s. To do so, make sure to have not just recent statements but three to four statements for each account (providing you didn't just shovel the funds into that account that month) in both original and photocopy. You´ll show them the original and provide them the photocopy for their records (if you don´t provide a photocopy, they´ll take your original). In the odd case that it really is a Nicaraguan company that is providing your source of funds, provide a notarized copy of its legal registration in the *Registro*

Mercancíl.

Proof of dependency on other person (if applicable): If you primary funding source is another person, which is to say someone else declares you as dependent, on your primary source of income is alimony payments, you must provide the above (savings statements, proof of funds) for that person as well a letter signed, translated, and notarized by a Nicaraguan notary stating your dependency and the economic agreement that binds you to that person (e.g. alimony). Note that the Nicaraguan government frown on this as a source of funding, and you can expect to be asked to do more to verify your financial viability.

Certified criminal record from your country of origin: You request this from your local police department back home. If you've moved around a lot, you need a record from every country in which you have resided for the past five years (if you've just traveled to a country but not resided there, it doesn't count). You request that letter from your police department, then present it to the Nicaraguan consulate so the staff can authenticate it. They return it to you with a stamp indicating they recognize the letter as a valid document, not a forgery. The embassy may require you have the document translated. If so, there will likely be an official translator in-house to do the work for you, for which you can expect to be charged.

Birth Certificate: This means your original birth certificate with a raised seal, as well as a photocopy for their records. Again, if you don´t provide a birth certificate for each of them as well as corresponding photocopies. These birth certificates must be authenticated by the Nicaraguan consulate in your home country and translated if the consulate requests it.

Marriage License:
If you are married to a non-Nicaraguan citizen, you need only present your marriage license to the Nicaraguan consulate in your home country to be authenticated (and translated if requested). If you are married to a Nicaraguan, you must provide the Nicaraguan marriage license and a copy of that person's *cédula*. Paradoxically, being married to a Nicaraguan requires more paperwork but encourages immigration to look upon your case more favorably: There is less perceived risk that you will disappear leaving bills unpaid. Emphasizing that point regularly throughout the process will smooth your way.

Certificate of Good Health:
You need a letter from a doctor in your native country declaring you to be in good health and free from communicable diseases. The Nicaraguan government isn't too concerned with whether you have arthritis or a bad back; it's looking for HIV/AIDS, typhoid, tuberculosis, and such. Have your doctor mention these things, specifically in the letter so there is no doubt whatsoever about the state of your physical health. This letter must be delivered to the Nicaraguan consulate nearest you to be authenticated and translated.

Carta de Baja:
Obtained from the Ministry of Foreign Relations (*Ministerio de Relaciones Exteriores, also called the cancillería*), this is sort of a note of approval and essentially involves the *cancillería* checking to make sure you are not a persona non grata on any official government lists. The *cancilleria* will request proof

of your having paid the necessary deposit before they provide you the *carta de baja*.

Cash Deposit:
The deposit is mandatory and provides the government of Nicaragua with the necessary fund to deport you if for any reason they find it necessary. The deposit is currently USD 2750 and covers the price of a fist-class airline ticket to anywhere in the western hemisphere, but expect that fee to raise at the whim of any director of immigration. You pay the fee into the Immigration Special deposit (Fondo especial de Migracíon) at the *Banco de la Producción* – and retain your receipt as proof of the deposit. You have no right to request this money be reimbursed unless you rescind your Nicaraguan residency, at which point you may ask for the money to be returned to you. It´s possible but not easy to do this. You will not receive any interest on the deposit.

Residency Fees:
A temporary resident visa costs about USD 1000 per year (this may amount will fluctuate each year). Try not to think about the fact5 that four 90-day tourist visas for the same period would´ve cost you USD 28 service fee.

Other Fees:
You must pay several additional documents-processing fees to a special office within Immigration called SERTAMI (*Sercvicio de Tramites de Inmigración*). These include USD 16 for the processing of your residence card (your *cédula*) and a USD 7 service fee. (this may amount will fluctuate each year).

Other Documents:

Officially, that´s the end of the paperwork. But be4 prepared to provide additional justification if your situation is not straightforward. IF you are a retiree living on a fixed income provided by your pension, you may or may not be required to provide an official *INTURISMO* declaration. If you are a student (which raises the question why you need permanent residency in Nicaragua), you will be required to provide proof of your university registration. And of course, the officials have the right to demand additional documents if they are not convinced by what you have provided.

Investor´s Visa ("Residency for Immigrants with Capital") The investor´s visa has the same requirements as above along with a few others. The most onerous is a certificate from the Ministry of Development, Industry, and Trade (*MIFIC, Ministerio de Fomento Industria y Comercio*) recognizing the business you intend to establish in Nicaragua. In practice this is tricky, but it´s not difficult given the government´s interest in encouraging foreign investment. MIFIC will evaluate your business plan, which should be in Spanish. Very few foreigners take advantage of the investor´s visa, and you cannot consider the purchase of your home or land in Nicaragua as an investment for the visa: It is intended for industrial and commercial entrepreneurs as well as anyone who intends to sustain himself or herself in Nicaragua on the proceeds of a business venture. You will need the following:

1.   **The certificate from MIFIC**
2.   **Bank Certificate**: This certificate from the relevant financial institution – usually the Nicaraguan Central Bank – but sometimes also the Treasury (*Ministerio de Hacienda y Credito Publico*) stating the amount of capital that will be invested in securities.

3.   Evidence of Income: You can provide this information in the same format you would for a Temporary Residence Visa, i.e. bank statements and similar documents.

Retiree Visa

In June 2009 the Law for the promotion of the **Retiree Residency** was passed (along with many other immigration laws), enacting provisions specifically designed for encouraging foreign retirees to make Nicaragua their new home. Law 694 as it´s known, provides the following benefits: no requirement for a guarantee bond (unlike the residency visas above) the right to import up to USD 20,000 of household effects tax-free (the car must not be older than seven years, and you cannot sell it without four years of its importation without having to pay a fee), a one-time exemption on importation of USD 50,000 worth of construction materials, sales-tax exemption for car rentals, and tax exemption on up to USD 200,000 of scientific or professional items if they will be used for the benefit of Nicaragua (doctors and dentists who want to bring your equipment, this provision is aimed squarely at you). Note that to take advantage of this law, you need to have a birth certificate (translated and notarized) showing your age of at least 45 years (if you are younger, you should have proof of an investment you have made in Nicaragua of at least USD 75,000). In addition to these documents, you must write a letter to the director general of INTUR requesting permission to retire in Nicaragua, with copies of all these documents and a list of all household items, vehicles, and other things you intend to import under this provision.

Here are some other benefits in a nutshell:
One of the benefits regarding tax and customs exemption is you can import of up to $20,000 in value of household goods. There is no sales tax (currently 15%) for first USD 50,000 of materials in building or restoring a home (up to $7,500 but you can't sell your property for 10 years)

The best source of information on the immigration laws and procedures is Nicaragua's own immigration site, but it is in Spanish.

http://www.migracion.gob.ni/

The Application Process (Updated 2018)

With the recent influx of investors and expats going through the immigration system, immigration into this country today is better of than it was in 2010 or before major reforms in 2005, but you still need to keep your patience. One reason things seem confusing is that many steps happen simultaneously, like your dealings with MIFIC and Immigration (if you are an investor), and other happen sequentially, like the airline ticket deposit, which must occur before the Ministry of Foreign Relations will grant you your *carta de baja*.

Begin the process by going to the Immigration building and requesting a form for the appropriate resident visa. The form is important, but more important is the opportunity to ask questions of the person who gives it to you – and for a printed list of all the steps required (they have these, so make sure you get one). Look it over and make sure the next steps are clear before leaving the building. At that point, you can begin the rest of the steps, like visiting the *Ministerio de Relaciones Exteriores*, placing the deposit in the *Banco de Producción*, and requesting authentication and translation services from your embassy, if necessary. When you have gathered all the required documents, return to Immigration to have them processed. The earlier in the day you get to the office, the better luck you will have (a good mantra for Nicaraguan bureaucracies in general).

The Judicial System and Hiring a Lawyer

Nicaragua is a democracy with all the usual institutions and the judicial system is leaned from the English with all its advantages and shortcomings. Generally, a foreigner should stay away from involvement in judicial processing, that means avoiding lawsuits, injury claims and lawsuits. The system is very corrupt and foreigner more often than not are ending up on the paying side not matter what the case is. Simple as that. Public confidence in the fairness of this system is extremely low and corruption and nepotism often prevail. Because of the corruption in the judicial system, entrepreneurs are generally advised to search alternative dispute resolutions including mediation

Hiring a lawyer

Looking at the mountains of paperwork that lies between you and official residency, it is tempting to retain the professional services of an attorney and indeed, many Nicaraguan attorneys are willing to help you with your residency paperwork. This is a recommended avenue if your Spanish is not good enough to deal confidently with the sort of Spanish you find on official documentation.
However, if you've spent enough time in Nicaragua to feel comfortable with the language and speak Spanish well enough to represent yourself in person before immigration authorities, an attorney might be of limited use. Instead consider taking along a Nicaraguan friend whenever you deal

with Immigration. Again, the subtle message of your ability to fit into Nicaraguan society and the suggestion that you might "know people" will be helpful, but more importantly, the cultural interpretation your friend will provide during the process can be very beneficial. Should you decide to contract a Nicaraguan attorney you can expect to pay USD 300 – 500 or more for his or her services.

Taxes

The governmental institution in charge of collecting taxes is called the *Dirección General de Ingresos* (DGI). Lacking computerization, a smooth organization, and manpower, the DGI has a hard time collecting taxes. A tax paying culture appears to be absent, and the DGI lacks control measures to make sure all businesses and citizens pay their fair share. Consequently, tax evasion is commonplace.

There are five income tax brackets, with tax rates varying from 0% to 25%. Below is an overview:
from (C$) to (C$) base tax (C$) tax rate

from (C$)	to (C$)	base tax (C$)	tax rate
1	50,000		0%
50,001	100,000		10%
100,001	200,000	min.5,000	15%
200,001	300,000	min.20,000	20%
300,001	and up	min.40,000	25%

Law 306 incentives extend into a variety of business types that are eligible for tax exemptions. For example, investing in environmentally protected areas, arts and crafts, transportation (land, water or air), or investment in infrastructure such as marinas, energy production, waste disposal treatment, and other such options, particularly hotels, bed and breakfasts, lodges, condos, etc. are also covered under this tax code. Many Nicaraguans are unemployed or earn low wages and thus the establishment of new businesses, especially those that can make use of personnel, is encouraged

A Word About the Economy

Since the beginning of the century Nicaragua's economic condition has improved substantially, but it is still a developing country and some visitors are initially shocked by the poverty they encounter there. Nicaragua is the second poorest country after Haiti in the Western Hemisphere. Still Nicaragua is rich in natural resources. The country has deposits of copper, gold, gypsum, iron ore, lead, silver and zinc.

Since the fast majority in Nicaragua is struggling, the harsh economy has deeply affected family structures. Despite all the economic difficulties that affect family stability, the Nicaraguan family sees itself as a monogamous unit. Nicaraguans tend to have large families, and Nicaragua is a young country: 40% of the population is under 15 years of age. Strong, affective family ties, and even dependence, are very strong between children, parents, brothers and sisters, aunts and uncles. However, economic factors reinforce these ties even in the wealthier classes.

Buying Real Estate in Nicaragua

Let me be frank, a lot of very stupid people coming to Nicaragua, thinking this country is the new *Eldorado* in the Western hemisphere; many foreigners who come here don't speak a word of Spanish, most don't even bother to get a lawyer, and just seem to trust someone they've known for a week enough to hand over money for some land. No matter what standards you have, this is crazy, but they seem to think it is okay in Nicaragua and then they write about it in blogs and give bad press.

If you are serious about buying real estate in Nicaragua, there are a lot of checks which need to be carried out which if done properly, ensure the safety of land ownership in Nicaragua - like a form stating that the property is free of any liens, a survey to make sure the land borders match what is held in the central registry so there is no confusion with who owns what; the seller needs to show a certificate named *carta de no objections* - this is most important and states that the property is able to be sold and no one in the government has any objections or rights to it - it is illegal to sell property now without this certificate, but it still gets done like this if a transaction is not done correctly.

What are Nicaraguans saying to the subject of buying property?

Many say they were once supporters of the Sandinistas, (The leftist government) that they always have been voting for Daniel Ortega. But times have changes, nowadays everyone hates Daniel Ortega and especially his agrarian reformists policies, because everybody know someone who had their property taken for agrarian reform.

Most people would never purchase property in a place where the citizens have lost their own property, knowing as a resident your holdings would be even more suspect. And knowing that many foreigners have hiked the prices to ridiculous levels for what you get in some areas there?

As you have probably gathered, there are official plans for a new canal connecting the Nicaragua Lake with the Pacific, needless to mention, one should stay clear of buying land anywhere between Managua to north of Granada.

If you talk with Nicaraguans now (2016), they would laugh if you said you were afraid that the government will take your land. Sure, they are working on straightening out some title issues, but issues like overlapping lots because of poor surveying techniques in the past happen in the US and Canada too. The overwhelming intent of the government is to attract investment to the country. The Nicaraguan government is officially very interested in making sure that developments of foreigners are a success, because it brings money and jobs while being eco-friendly. Nicaragua has some of the most protected natural reserve land in Central America and if they can get help with continuing that while helping their economy through jobs and investment they are very keen on it.

Business Ideas Suitable for Nicaragua

No idea is perfect, but the following business ideas are based on my personal experience as well as investigations of what might be possible in this country with a relatively good chance of success.
Available as an ebook on various book platforms:

111 Modern Business Ideas for Expats: Start Over Abroad 111 Business Startup Ideas for Anyone Everywhere

Open a Diving School
Renting land and real estate in general is still cheap in Nicaragua compared to neighboring countries. In neighboring Costa Rica you have fierce local competition plus complicated license procedures that can be a challenging enterprise even

though profit margins are still high. In Nicaragua it's different; small beach towns like *San Juan de Sur* and *Las Penitas* are getting more popular every year; prices and rents are still reasonable, and on the Atlantic coast north of *Bluefields* (where English is spoken) you find incredibly good deals for beach shops and storefronts (just be careful with whom your dealing with), the water is pristine with some acceptable good coral reefs just offshore; I suspect it will be only a question of a short time before tourism will become fully developed in that area.

The location of a diving school is very important; you should seek a highly visible shop close to the water but at the same time you need to avoid high rents. This is a long-term business and can require a substantial investment, so don't invest in any area that shows strong signs of decline in tourism, too many beach bumps or show massive corruption.

Import Exclusive Liquors
Even Nicaragua has many liquor shops and supermarkets that sell alcohol, it still can be frightening how few variety is actually available.
Import a number of hart-to-get liquors such as fruit schnaps, exclusive vodka, whiskey and tequila, and show them via your iPad to restaurant owners.

In most countries, you have to pay import duty on "premium packed spirits" (PPS) and the procedure to obtain an import license is sometimes not out of this world yet it's something not for the faint of heart. Start small, you can buy directly from importers; for your bar customers, you will be "a person of interest".

Offer Special Educational Tours
In Nicaragua and Central America in general, that would be coffee and tobacco plantation tours and if you happen to live near the Managua it could be local jewelry factories. Generally, most alcoholic beverage producers are very helpful to arrange tour packages. A very low-cost startup alternative would be just to promote the in-house tours of the manufacturer and you get your commission from them.

A good book on educational tours is Alison L. Grinder's "The Good Guide: A Sourcebook for Interpreters, Docents, and Tour Guides"

Importing Cosmetics and Natural Products
Importing and distributing natural products and cosmetics; this can be an excellent business opportunity if you can get it marketed correctly. Usually you would need to have a license for the imports and registration for each class of product. Especially in Latin America this can be a headache, and you

are in fierce competition with cheap brands from China. On the other hand, you have a huge amount of shops, and business owners who are very aware of the superior quality of Western natural products.

TV advertising and printing material is incredibly cheap in Nicaragua! You just have to convince the manufacturer in your home country to support you with all the paperwork and red tape. Once you have the products inside the country, registered, and you have bought enough TV and radio advertising, most likely your business will grow and expand.

Fugitives Escapists Paradise Nicaragua?

In this section I am not talking about asylum seekers, and political refugees, however one can generally describe a refuge as a person who has to flee his native country in order to escape prosecution from his home country. Nowadays there are many reasons of why a person has to leave his/her home country and find a new place to live and to be save from the authorities who are following and searching for the refugee. The most common reasons are:

- Criminal prosecution and issued warrants for his arrest.
- Tax evasion
- Political and religious prosecution in his/her home country
- Outstanding debt that makes life in his/her home country impossible.

Those are the most obvious reasons but more than often there are "normal" people, regular folks who are just seeking a new life in privacy; people who are looking for a complete change of culture and mentality. Nowadays many people from all over the world have become tired and uncomfortable with nosy, paranoid governments and bureaucrats in their home country.

Nicaragua is a fairly good place to start a new life and to live relatively safe "under the radar".
Nicaragua has extradition agreements with most Western countries and is working closely with Interpol. But unless you are a wanted terrorist or major drug-dealer, the Nicaraguan government and its authorities are usually not interested in actively searching for foreigners and tourists who have fled their native country for whatever reason.

By the time of writing the Nicaraguan government is still "leftist", has a political and military alliance with Cuba and is the "yes and amen" corner of the infamous dictatorship in Venezuela. Nicaragua has generally not too much interest in working with authorities from the USA or the EU.

As long as you are not a "high profile case", and you are not already in the system of Interpol, it is highly unlikely that you will not get your 3 month tourist stamp at the immigration office at the airport in Managua. (Assuming the refugee is traveling with his/her original passport) But it must be said that, generally speaking, it is not advisable getting involved in the immigration process if you are a refuge (some underpaid official might still take his research in your application a bit too serious and stir up unnecessary attention). And as a general rule, a refuge should always stay away from any official, keep a low profile, avoid other foreigners and change his/her destination and place of living as much as possible. Assuming a temporary new identity and knowledge of the language of the new home country is a "must and minimum" for any refugee.

Outside of the capital of Managua the *Migracion* (immigration police) is regularly checking almost every hotel, to investigate the bookings of foreigners as well as all guests they can find on the premise! They also checking on foreigners on the street; so it is wise to carry at least a photocopy of your passport otherwise you might be temporarily arrested until they can verify your identity. After all Nicaragua is country with a "half communist government- regime" that has a tradition on spying on their own citizens, and foreigners are no exception to this practice.

One area of interest for a refugee in Nicaragua might be the Caribbean cost around *Bluefields* and *Puerto Cabezas* and the eastern part of the country. Here you find a very different culture and mentality, the inhabitants understand English (they speak it very different and their native language is Creole), have a different history and don´t want to have much to do with any authorities from Managua. Traditionally it is an almost inaccessible land and has given refuge to many "undesirables" in the past such as Colombian drug runners and merchandise smugglers. On the other hand, this area is still fairly undeveloped with its share of crime and violence. Very few foreigners dare to live here, but those who succeed can have a more anonymous life then in most places in the region.

Trivial Information & Location

Some foreigners who have visited the country would argue that there is not enough quality lifestyle in Nicaragua to enjoy. Then again others would say that local life and local entertainment is vibrant and colorful. The differences in opinion are understandable since Nicaragua's social life, entertainment and nightlife options change from city to city and it all depends on where you go and who you know. In terms of entertainment you cannot compare Nicaragua with Costa Rica or even Honduras, matter-of-fact, it´s still a rather underdeveloped socialist third-world-country, yet with its own charm and opportunities.

Before I wrote this report, quite a few curious expats have asked me to write about the nightlife for expats in Nicaragua. Except for the little town of Granada and San Juan de Sur there is not that much, however there are a variety of options available and what you choose will generally depend on your taste in entertainment.

Some cities have a thriving disco and club scene for students and backpackers whilst a few areas such as Granada and San Juan de Sur feature local theatrical performances and picturesque restaurant dining. Still others feature virtually no nightlife at all and focus on relaxing evenings by the fireplace or on the balcony whilst nursing your beverage of choice. It is good to keep in mind that the lifestyle here is generally quite laid back. Granada is a popular choice with tourists due to its architectural heritage. If you visit this town, you will find that there is quite an active nightlife near the end of *'La Calzada'* Avenue by the shore of Lake Nicaragua. Perhaps the best feature here is a boulevard where you can enjoy pleasant evening strolls. The *'Centro Turistico'* features restaurants, beaches and discos for those looking for something more lively. As a resort town, *Montelimar* has endless activities to enjoy during the evening. You can swim whilst sipping a cocktail from the beach bar, go gambling at the casino, enjoy fine dining or join the local and visiting youth at the discotheque. *Puerto Cabezas* features four disco clubs which are open almost every day of the week. Clubs are usually busiest and at their best on weekends and during the holidays seasons.

Managua is still recovering from extensive damaged caused by an earthquake, but that does not mean it has nothing to offer. It may not be the ideal for club-seeking younger adventurers, but it does offer those with a taste for culture two fine options. Firstly, right near the city center in one of the original, undamaged buildings called the Fine Arts Palace. Managua has several modern *Centro Comerciales*, a few simple bars which call themselves pubs and some outdoor cafes near and around the Hilton, not to mention a few half rundown and overpriced nightclubs catering to local yuppies and corporate men with a few hundred Dollar spare money to burn.

The small town of *Rivas* has a few fine (some argue "decent") restaurants which make for a great evening out. If you want to enjoy some local music, there is a local disco (in this country it is not uncommon for elderly men to go to a disco "just to watch the crowd") For something calmer, you might try seeing a movie at the cinema but check first to see what language the films are being shown in. If you're really looking for entertainment, it might be a good idea to visit Nicaragua during one of the major festivals when the towns come alive.

Nicaragua is arguably not the most beautiful but the hottest of all the Central American countries. If you prefer to live among other expats, the hot little town of Granada is a place where most expats and foreign pensioners gather. Many foreigners prefer this little enclave to start a small business.

Generally speaking, if your Spanish is good enough Nicaragua has plenty of small to medium size business opportunities; licenses are comparable ease to obtain and compared to neighboring countries Nicaragua produces and exports a rather large number of products and articles. Many expats are doing well in the hospitality and gastronomy due to the fact that experience, knowledge and talent is still a precious commodity in this country. Nicaragua is an option for people on a medium budget with an acceptable level of risk.

International Healthcare

If you're being sent overseas by your multinational employer, its health plan may travel with you. If you are not covered by an employer, and if you are not a citizen or covered by a private healthcare provider of this country, most likely you won´t be qualified for the national healthcare plan in your host country even if it has a universal health care system.

Many foreigners "on their own" are not properly insured and will pay medical bills to a local doctor or in case of an emergency they have to present a credit card at the nearest hospital, however many realize with time that they are better off to buy their own international "expat" insurance.
'

For your reference, I have collected some international medical insurance providers:

Insubuy Inc.
4700 Dexter Dr. Suite 100
Plano, TX 75093
USA
(972) 985 4400
Email: bai73@insubuy.com

International Medical Group
2960 North Meridian Street
Indianapolis, IN USA 46208-4715
Telephone: 1.317.655.4500 or 1.800.628.4664
Fax: 1.317.655.4505

IHI International Health Insurance danmark (Dänemark)
http://global.ihi.com/
Palaegade 8, DK-1261 Kopenhagen K, Danmark
Tel.: +45 33 15 30 99, FAX: +45 33 32 25 60
Email: ihi@ihi.com

InterGlobal Insurance Company Limited (England)

http://www.interglobalpmi.com
Woolmead House East, The Woolmead, Farnham, Surrey, GU9 7TT, United Kingdom
From Thailand, call free on Tel.: 001 800 647 355
Tel.: +44 (0) 1252 745 965, Fax: +44 (0) 1252 745 920
Email: clientservices@interglobalpmi.com

AXA PPP healthcare (England)
http://www.axappphealthcare.co.uk/international-health-insurance
Phillips House, Crescent Road, Tunbridge Wells, Kent, TN1 2PL, United Kingdom
Tel. +44 (0) 1892 708 101

HealthCare International Global Network Ltd
UK Administration
95 Cromwell Road
London SW7 4DL
United Kingdom
enquiries@healthcareinternational.com
For general claims enquiries, please email
claims@healthcareinternational.com

Bupa International (England)
http://www.bupa-intl.com
Russell House, Russell Mews, Brighton BN1 2NR, United Kingdom
Tel: +44 (0)1273 323 563 , Fax: +44 (0)1273 820517
Email: http://www.bupa-intl.com/bupaintlhome/for-you/personal-contact

DKV Globality S.A. (Luxemburg)
http://www.dkv-globality.com/de/
13, rue Edward Steichen, L-2540 Luxembourg
Tel.: +352/ 270 444-1000, Telefax: +352/ 270-9000
Email: contact@dkv-globality.com

Allianz Worldwide Care Ltd. (Irland)
www.allianzworldwidecare.com
18B Beckett Way, Park West Business Campus, Nangor Road, Dublin 12, Ireland

Conclusion and Afterword

My ideas and suggestions aren't magic, they are the result of my worldwide experience with all sorts of businesses and of a way of thinking and analyzing those businesses which already have been proven successful in many developing countries.

Anyone who wishes to establish himself in a foreign country is well advised to offer products or services that have a correlation to their respective home country. Means, if you are from the US your business needs be typical and of positive remembrance to America. Generally, you shouldn't start a business that would be "a-typcial" to your background. For example, if you are British don't run a Chinese restaurant and if you are Swiss don't start a comedy club; in most third world countries people have a simple cliché of foreigners, and somehow you and your business need to fit into their "worldview" because it makes it easier for people to recognize you as an "expert". Nicaragua is not a rich country, however,more likely than not, your best customers will most likely be well connected locals.

In third world countries security is always an issue, therefore, I do not recommend any business that makes you vulnerable, susceptible to blackmail or in any way a potential target to crooks and gangs. Especially if you plan to open a shop or permanent office, stay away from any product or business that looks remotely valuable to uneducated angry men who might bear grudges against foreigners.

Thank you for buying my book. I wish you good luck and all the best with your future endeavors in Nicaragua; if you found this book useful I'd greatly appreciate if you would post me a positive review, your support and feedback does make a difference and it helps spreading a positive message about the country. Thanks again.

Made in the USA
Las Vegas, NV
10 November 2023

80600739R00031